Pullman Company

The Story of Pullman

Pullman Company

The Story of Pullman

ISBN/EAN: 9783742840691

Manufactured in Europe, USA, Canada, Australia, Japa

Cover: Foto ©Thomas Meinert / pixelio.de

Manufactured and distributed by brebook publishing software
(www.brebook.com)

Pullman Company

The Story of Pullman

I.

THE Pullman World's Fair exhibit is unique. It is unique in the fact that what it represents is in its entire development, as well as its origin, distinctively and purely American. It is the evolution of an idea originated by an American, in a wholly new field of progress in which there had not been even any tentative gropings in other lands than ours, and by an American worked out along lines of strong individual personality, until it has overshadowed and revolutionized all other methods everywhere in the area of its operation.

It is an interesting fact in connection with the Pullman Exhibition train that it holds precisely the same position in its particular field that was held by the first Pullman car ever built. The first Pullman car, at the time it was completed, represented the Nineteenth century's highest achievement in the machinery of travel, just as unquestionably as does the train of Pullmans exhibited at the Columbian Exposition of 1893. Not only that, but there has never been a time, from the completion of that first car to the completion of the World's Fair train, when the Pullman car was not the Nineteenth century's highest achievement in vehicles for passenger transportation. During all the years from the beginning of the Pullman work to the present day, it has never been dislodged from the dominant position it took in one leap at the very outset. Had a World's Fair been held every year, from that in which the old Pioneer, the first of the great Pullman fleet of traveling palaces, was launched, to the year in which we live, the best the century had done in solving the problem of long journeyings by land would always have been the latest car turned out from the Pullman shops.

Of the material benefits to humanity which this achievement has brought, the beautiful train of World's Fair cars is the expression. It speaks for itself; needs no interpreter. But there is more than a material side to what has been accomplished. In the building up of the Pullman industries, what may be termed pure abstract sentiment has played a greater part than is commonly known. Appreciation of the value of the beautiful has not found expression merely in making sleeping-car interiors the object-lessons in decorative art that they are. That which is harmonious and beautiful has been recognized as having an incitive energy of its own, capable in its way of being turned to account as a force in the production of results, just as is the force of the steam engine itself. It is as a symbol of this, to a certain extent, that the World's Fair model of the Town of Pullman has significance. But the Town of Pullman means more than that. It is a product, and perhaps may prove to be the culminating product in its enduring benefits to mankind, of the principles on which the entire Pullman fabric is reared. Its growth is as much the logical outcome of those principles as is the palace car train itself.

To understand this, to know something of how one man has been able to create a vast productive industry, which is one of the century's great civilizing strides, and which, from small beginnings has now reached a market value of $60,000,000, it is necessary to get back to the beginning of the undertaking, and to follow briefly the outline of its development.

GREEN STONE CHURCH

II.

At just what time Mr. Pullman first began thinking on the subject of sleeping-cars, he would himself perhaps find it difficult to tell. The problem had been raised by the completion of what then were considered long lines of railroad. Baltimore, Philadelphia and New York had thrown out filaments of iron for considerable distances toward the West. To get to the Ohio River at either Wheeling or Pittsburgh, or to get to Lake Erie at Dunkirk or Buffalo, involved a journey of over 400 miles. A journey of 400 miles took as much time as now does one of more than double that distance. The physical fatigue involved was greater than is now incident to a trip from the Atlantic Ocean to the Pacific.

With the increase of competition there had come an increase in the public demands. Roads began to make efforts to increase travel by introducing devices to promote the traveler's comfort, and certain clumsy attempts were made to provide him a sort of bunk in which he could get a little sleep at night.

Mr. Pullman was at that time a young man. In a general way, the sleeping-car and its possibilities had floated through his mind, and he had casually discussed the matter with friends. His first serious attention to it, however, dates from a certain night journey he made about that time from Buffalo to Westfield. It was a sixty-mile ride, and he occupied a bunk in one of the so-called sleeping-cars of that epoch. During the journey he lay awake, revolving in his mind plans by which the car could be transformed into a dormitory, in which there would be a greater degree of comfort and elegance. While it cannot be said that his determination to make sleeping-car construction the occupation of his life dates from that particular night's ride, it is certain that he left the train at Westfield convinced that he could build a better car than the one he had just occupied, and dimly seeing, even thus early, the possibility of there being in that direction a field for his life-work.

But it was not until some time after this, that he entered into the subject in earnest. His reflections had then convinced him that in the sleeping-car lay the solution of the problem of long continuous journeys, which in the near future was destined to become among the most important to the traveling public of any growing out of the rapid expansion of the American system of railroads. During the years from 1859 to 1863, he made a series of experiments on the Chicago & Alton and the old Galena roads. From these experiments, which involved not only his own devices but the suggestions of patents then existing, he had worked out detailed plans which he set about putting into execution on a thorough and comprehensive basis. A workshop was rented and skilled mechanics employed. Mr. Pullman threw himself into the task with the ardor of a man who moves from settled convictions. Although he was without mechanical training himself, he personally directed the work of others in all the minute details of putting the ideas he had originated into material form.

The result of many months of hard, loyal labor was the car Pioneer. The place the Pioneer at once took as the most per-

MAIN ADMINISTRATION BUILDING.

LAKE VISTA.

fect railway vehicle the world, up to that time, had ever seen, has been already mentioned. How great was the gap between it and the best that had gone before is indicated by the comparative cost. The best sleeping-cars in use before the Pioneer had cost $4,000 each. The Pioneer cost $18,000. That was a tremendous leap forward. It was a revolution in all existing theories of car construction. The new car was a radical departure, not only in respect of weight and solidity, but also in the elaborate and artistic nature of its interior fittings and decorations. In both of these respects it was adversely criticised. That massive strength combined with striking beauty of ornamentation and minute elaboration of every device for comfort, which all the world now recognize as the highest distinctive merits of the Pullman cars, was the very point which at the outset was most strenuously objected to.

It is time that tells in the case of all great progressive innovations, and in the light of what time has told us who live in this last decade of the century, it is instructive as well as amusing to recall the grounds on which the first application of the Pullman principles in car building were condemned.

We know now that men will not climb in between the sheets of a Pullman sleeping-car bed with their boots on, and that they will not regard sleeping-car carpets and upholstery in the light of convenient cuspidors. We know that the same instinct which makes people conform in their habits to elegant surroundings in homes, will make them proportionately conform to them in public vehicles. We know that the beautiful interiors of Pullman cars, which were once condemned as absurd extravagance, have now a commercial value, which men are not only willing to pay for, but have come to demand, and that they therefore are a profitable financial investment. We know, too, that probably from no other one source has there sprung so widely diffused an education, so general an ambition in the direction of interior decorative art, the effect of which is seen in thousands of American homes to-day, as has come from the beautiful object-lessons which these cars have carried to the remotest regions of the country.

All this we know, now that it has been demonstrated to us, just as well as we know that the massive weight and strength of the Pullman car have saved hundreds of lives in railway disasters, and that the Pullman standard of weight, solidity, and beauty of ornamentation has set the pace which has been followed in the construction of the passenger cars in use upon all the roads of the country. Indeed, the best types of all passenger vehicles in operation to-day in the United States, might properly be included in the Pullman World's Fair exhibit of results accomplished, for the reason that they are as distinctively the outcome of Pullman ideas and the public demand which is the result of those ideas, as are the Pullman cars themselves.

It is not to be understood that the criticisms of the Pioneer were universally adverse. On the contrary, the car attracted wide attention, and was enthusiastically admired. Its superiority over anything ever before built was too obvious to be unrecognized. The objection found to it was the vital one that it would not pay. The fact was that the stride forward was too sudden, too great a shock to existing theories for even the most progressive railway men to follow at once to its real significance.

MAIN ADMINISTRATION BUILDING.

HOTEL FLORENCE.

THE ARCADE.

The Pullman idea in particular, that money could be safely invested in an elaboration of the utilitarian into the artistic and beautiful, was a startling departure. The American citizen, it was assumed, had a sovereign contempt for anything, especially in the applied sciences, which in the slightest degree stepped over the baldest utility into the boundaries of the ornamental. If you gave him the substantial with artistic surroundings and beautiful accessories, the assumption was that it was reasonably certain he would expectorate on the surroundings and wipe his boots on the accessories. It was certain he would never pay for either the one or the other.

That was practically the theory on which railway passenger cars were constructed prior to the building of the Pioneer. It was erroneous, of course, as the Pioneer and its immediate successors demonstrated. Yet the crudity of public taste in the United States at that time as contrasted with the present day is sufficiently apparent. There is no more striking illustration of this than comes from a comparison of the architecture of the decade of 1850-60 with that of the decade in which we are now living. The progress in artistic development made in the interval by the people of the whole country which this contrast reveals, is truly remarkable; and it is quite within bounds to say that one at least of the influences which have brought about this result, is the sincere efforts in that line which have marked every stage of progress in the Pullman work.

In his own field Mr. Pullman was in reality the pioneer in this element of progress. He was a believer in the beautiful, and he believed earlier than others whose dealings were with the public, that the American people would pay their money for it and respect it in a public vehicle as well as in a

private home. How firmly he nailed his colors to this convic-
tion he demonstrated in the very next car he built. Into the
Pioneer he put more than four times as much money as had
ever gone into the construction of any car it succeeded.
Into the Pioneer's successor he put six times as much. The
Pioneer cost $18,000; the car which came after it cost $24,000.

It was on the Michigan Central Railway that the Pioneer's
immediate successors were first run. Mr. Joy, the President
of that line when the new Pullmans were put on, was one of
the progressive railroad men of the day, and he had caught
the meaning of the Pullman work and had seen in it practi-
cal possibilities. But even he had his doubts when the conditions under which the new cars must be run were presented
to him. Their largely increased cost necessitated an increased
tariff for berths. The price of a berth in the old cars was
$1.50. It was impracticable to sell a berth in a car that had cost
$24,000 for less than two dollars. The increase, President Joy
said, could not be attempted. The additional fifty cents
would drive night-travel from his road to competing lines.

Mr. Pullman suggested that the matter be submitted to the
decision of the traveling public. He proposed that the new
cars, with their increased rate, be put on trains with the old
cars at the cheaper rate. If the traveling public thought the
beauty of finish, the increased comfort and the safety of the
new cars worth two dollars per night, there were the $24,000
cars; if, on the other hand, they were satisfied with less
attractive surroundings at a saving of fifty cents, the cheaper
cars were at their disposal. It was a simple submission without
argument of the plain facts on both sides of the issue—in other
words, an application of the good American doctrine of appeal-

THE ARCADE.

ing to the people as the court of highest resort. The decision came instantly and in terms which left no opening for discussion. The only travelers who rode in the old cars were those who were grumbling because they could not get berths in the new ones. After running practically empty for a few weeks, the cars in which the price for a berth was $1.50 were withdrawn from service, and Pullmans, wherein the two-dollar tariff prevailed, were substituted in their places, and this for the very potent reason that the public insisted upon it. Nor did the results stop there. The Michigan Central Railway, charging an extra tariff of fifty cents per night as compared with other Eastern lines, proved an aggressive competitor of those lines, not in spite of the extra charge, but because of it and of the higher order of comfort and beauty it represented.

Then followed a curious reversal of the usual results of competition. Instead of a leveling down to the cheaper basis on which all opposition was united, there was a leveling up to the standard on which the Pullman service was planted and on which it stood out single-handed and alone. Within comparatively a short period all the Michigan Central's rival lines were forced by sheer pressure from the traveling public to withdraw the inferior and cheaper cars and meet the superior accommodations and the necessarily higher tariff.

In other words, the inspiration of that key-note of vigorous ambition for excellence of the product itself, irrespective of immediate financial returns, which was struck with such emphasis in the building of the Pioneer, and which ever since has rung through all the Pullman work, was felt in the railroad world of the United States at that early date just as it is even more dominantly felt at the present time. At one bound it put the American railway passenger service in the leadership of all nations in that particular branch of progress, and has held it there ever since as an object-lesson in the illustration of a broad and far-reaching principle.

III.

Mr. Pullman had the good fortune to bring to the task
he had undertaken an ambition free from the fever of rapid
wealth-getting. He had within him, to a marked degree, the
creative instinct, the instinct which finds its highest gratification
in the thing itself that is created; which puts that always
first, leaving the financial results to follow in their proper
place, as incidents and corollaries of the main proposition.
He never at any stage of his progress entertained the idea
of turning the results he accomplished into a speculation. A
voyage to the illusive shores which border the oft-navigated
sea of watered stock never entered into his calculations. His
entire energies were concentrated upon the work itself, and
upon its constant improvement. Indeed that which from the
first has kept the integrity of the Pullman prestige, may be
described as a chronic dissatisfaction with that which has
been. The persistent effort to do something better than has
ever been done before, which sent the first Pullman car leagues
ahead of anything that had preceded it, has never for a mo-
ment been relaxed. In all the early contracts with railroad
companies, there was provided a margin to devote to efforts
toward this constant betterment.

It is this spirit which has made the Pullman work through-
out its entire development a progressive series of revelations,
many of them almost as striking as was the revelation in travel
possibilities which the Pioneer itself represented. Gradually

---

in this way the traveling-hotel idea was expanded. It was Mr. Pullman who taught the world that you can take a luxurious meal at the rate of fifty miles an hour, just as it was he who has made it possible for a man to do a day's work in one city, and rise refreshed and ready for another day's work in another city nearly a thousand miles away. It is an interesting speculation as to how much this, by multiplying many times the working capacity of the individual, has added to the total industrial energy of the country.

The hotel feature on the Pullman train was itself developed and improved upon until it reached its culmination in that exclusively Pullman device, the vestibule, which makes a solid yet perfectly sinuous train with practically absolute immunity from danger to passengers in even the most violent collision, and with the striking result of an entire train under one roof, in which the traveler may pass from his dining-room to his sitting-room, or to his sleeping-room, as in his own home.

How startling was the revelation made by this bold and original departure, is sufficiently shown by the almost universal adoption of it, or of substitutes which were close imitations of external appearances only, containing such features as might be used in technical avoidance of the Pullman patents, but lacking the essence of the invention which gives it its greatest value—the frictional contact for preventing oscillation, and the greater strength in resisting the shocks of collision.

With the possible exception of the invention of the air-brake, which puts the control of the train so completely into the hands of the engineer, there has been no event of railway development so important in securing safety to the traveling public as the invention of the Pullman vestibule. In its latest

application, as illustrated by the World's Fair train, it is extended to the locomotive tender itself, thus taking into its protecting arms not only the passengers, but the employes in the baggage and mail cars as well; and this extension is so constructed as to act as a wind-deflector, thus diminishing atmospheric resistance to the speed of trains.

The vestibule feature has also been enlarged in the Pullman Exhibition train to the full width of the cars, by extending the sides of the cars and enclosing the ends, together with an original and ingenious arrangement of vestibule entrance doors, and trap-doors over the steps. This materially adds to the comfort of passengers by doing away with the "wind pockets" which are formed by the ordinary projecting hoods over open platforms; and, furthermore, provides a comfortable and protected place for brakemen or other train employes whose duties may require them to ride occasionally upon platforms.

It is barely six years since the vestibule was invented, yet it has become so firmly fixed a feature of railway appliances that it has in reality given a new word to the English language. The term "vestibuled train" has passed into accepted use wherever English is spoken.

But the making of the best cars that had been known was but a preliminary step toward building up the Pullman service such as we know it to-day. We now start out from a city in the United States, Canada or Mexico, and we travel to all accessible parts of the North American continent, and everywhere, over hundreds of different railroads, we find the one harmonious, perfectly administered system of transportation. You may go aboard a Pullman car in New York or Chicago, and you may go aboard one in the wilds of Arizona, and in either case you find the same beautiful surroundings, the same cleanliness and order, the same comfort and attentive service. It is like one vast ubiquitous hotel, this Pullman service, which you may enter anywhere and in which you may go anywhere, taking your slippered ease in your inn as you go.

What of labor and tact and diplomatic gift it has required to build up all this, is comparatively little appreciated. We now and then marvel at the beauty and comfort of the particular shuttle which we occupy in its swift flight, but the great complicated mechanism of travel which spreads all over the continent, and of which our own particular shuttle is only a detail doing its appointed part—all this we accept as a matter of course. If we think of it at all, it is with the vague general impression that it is a natural evolution, a problem which somehow worked its own way out.

To demonstrate that the objections to the first Pullman car were groundless was a much easier task than to convince railroad men that it was only through an administration extraneous to any one road, or group of roads, that the best results to the railroads and to the public from the operation of those cars were to be obtained. The cars themselves carried their own argument, told their own story. The operating system came only gradually into evidence. Railroad men, with their minds concentrated on the development and administration of their own lines, had not given sufficient attention to the matter of long continuous runs to enable them quite to grasp the subject. The building up of such a system, they said, was impracticable. The interests involved were too conflicting, it was argued, ever to be harmonized. At the very best such a system would hang upon the slender thread of con-

tracts, and contracts would expire. Besides this, if the business should prove profitable, each railroad would insist upon operating its own sleeping-car and parlor-car services.

As a matter of fact, all the difficulties in the way of carrying out the project which were predicted for it, as well as many more which were not predicted, actually did present themselves and had to be overcome. There were two forces which constantly pushed the Pullman plan toward success. The plan, to begin with, was the logically correct one. In addition to that, the public was being steadily educated up to demand a standard of excellence in car equipment which just one concern produced, and that was the Pullman Company. The constant evolution by that company of striking material improvements and new beauties of design and ornamentation, kept a wide gap between it and the entire field of imitators which had sprung up in opposition. It was a contest to be decided on its merits alone, and the deciding power was fast slipping from the hands of the railroads to the hands of the public. The public had demonstrated not only that it would pay for the best, but that it would demand the best, and with competition at the point which it had now reached, the public demands were not to be slighted.

Then came the completion of the great Pacific line across the continent. Here was the problem of long continuous journeys presented in its most striking form. Almost simultaneously with the completion of the Pacific road, there was put upon the rails one of the most superb trains ever turned out of the Pullman shops. Its journey to California and its reception there, were in the nature of a progress and an ovation. From that time forth the great population of the Pacific coast knew no train for long-distance travel save a Pullman train, and would hear of no other. When people from California reached Chicago on their way eastward, the road over which Pullman cars ran got their patronage, and roads over which other cars were operated did not. Newspapers and magazines were awakened anew to studies of the Pullman cars and the Pullman system, and scores of printed pages were filled with the marvels of a journey to the Pacific ocean, which was nothing more than a six days' sojourn in a luxurious hotel, past the windows of which there constantly flowed a great panoramic belt of the American continent thousands of miles in length, and as wide as the eye could reach. Illustrated magazine articles which appeared, telling the story of a trip to California, had as many pictures of Pullman interiors as they had of the big trees or the Yosemite Valley.

The effect of all this was far-reaching. The great Pennsylvania line abandoned its own service and adopted the Pullman. The companies operating the sleeping-car and parlor-car services on the New York Central and Lake Shore systems made application for the privilege of using the Pullman plans, and were permitted to do so upon payment of stipulated royalties, which continued for many years, and until the expiration of the Pullman patents. Other opposition lines were absorbed, and the Pullman system and the Pullman cars established at last as we now know them, when the very name Pullman has become a synonymous and interchangeable term for the sleeping-car and the sleeping-car service. Its fleet has grown from one car to 2,500; its working force from half a dozen men to 15,000. Its cars are operated over nearly a hundred roads, and over a mileage equivalent to five times the circumference of the globe.

From the first year of its existence it has paid its quarterly
dividends with the regularity of a government loan, and its
$30,000,000 of capital has a market value of $60,000,000, while
its stock is so largely sought as a rock-ribbed security for the
investment of the funds of educational and charitable institu-
tions, of women and of trust estates, that out of its 3,246 stockholders, 1,800 are of this class, and 1,494 of these 1,800 are
women.

IV.

The story of Pullman naturally divides itself into three parts—the building of the car, the building up of the operating system, and the building of the town. Each of these stages is the natural, logical sequence of the other; through them all there runs the same underlying thought, the same thread of ideas.

The Pullman Palace Car Company suffered, as did all other industries, during the financial depression immediately following 1873, but the reaction which came on the heels of that gloomy era, on the resumption, in 1879, of specie payments, developed a rapid expansion of the Company's business. To meet this expansion and to extend the business still further along the line of general car-building and of other collateral industries, it became necessary to enlarge the plant. Its shops in St. Louis, Detroit, Elmira and Wilmington were unable to keep pace with the growing volume of demand for the company's productions. New shops must be built on a larger and more comprehensive scale than any that had gone before.

Chicago, with its central position with reference to the railway system of the continent, was obviously the natural site, but there were weighty objections, touching both finance and the matter of labor, to be urged against building within the limits of the city proper.

ARCADE THEATRE

To meet these objections and to have at the same
time the advantage of Chicago's geographical position and
great focus of railway connections, Mr. Pullman fixed upon
the vicinity of Lake Calumet, fourteen miles away. Here he
purchased 3,500 acres which has since increased in value proportionately with Chicago's remarkable development. The
entire tract is now embraced within the boundary limits of the
great city. Already the advance waves of Chicago's swelling
tide of population are lapping its edges and encircling its
borders. Even now, the Pullman district is a center around
which there is a connected girdle of thickly populated com-
munities. At a very early date the beautiful town of Pullman,
with its shaded avenues, its glimpses of bright water, its harmonious groupings of tasteful homes and churches and public
buildings, the whole colored here and there with the green of
lawns and the bloom of clustered banks of flowers—at a very
early date all this will be as a bright and radiant little island in
the midst of the great tumultuous sea of Chicago's population; a restful oasis in the wearying brick-and-mortar waste of
an enormous city.

And then, too, at its very door will come, not long hence,
the bulk of Chicago's manufacturing commerce. It is only a
matter of a short time when Lake Calumet, along which
the Pullman land stretches for miles, will become an inside har-
bor. The thirty million bricks per year which the Pullman
company is now manufacturing are made of clay taken from
the bottom of the lake, and in the meantime the Government
is dredging out the river which connects Calumet with the
thousands of miles of waterway of the great chain of lakes
which lead to the ocean and to the world beyond seas.

What this land, which a dozen years ago was bleak, sodden prairie, will represent when this comes to pass, and great ships are moored to its miles of water front, is an interesting item in speculations upon the marvelous probabilities of Chicago's future growth. The day is not only coming, but is near at hand when the $30,000,000 present capital stock of the Pullman Company will be covered, and more than covered, by the value of the 3,500 acres of land on which is built the town of Pullman.

Of the details of how Pullman was constructed; of how the dreary, water-soaked prairie was raised to high and dry land; of how the entire town was planned and blocked out in all its symmetrical unity of purpose by Mr. Pullman himself; of how the architect and landscape engineer, working together, carried out the details of the plan to their harmonious and beautiful conclusion—all this has been told and retold in the scores of studies of Pullman which have appeared in print on both sides of the Atlantic.

In the same publications there have appeared minute descriptions of the system by which the sewage of the town is collected and pumped far away to the Pullman produce farm; of how every house and flat, even to the cheapest in rent, is equipped with the modern appliances of water, gas, and internal sanitation; of how grounds for athletic sports were made ; all the merchandising of the town concentrated under the glass roof of a beautiful arcade building; a market house erected that is the ornament of one of the handsomest squares in the town; churches built; a beautiful schoolhouse put up, in which there attend nearly a thousand scholars; a library founded of over 8,000 volumes; a savings bank

MAIN GATE TO WORKS.

established, paying a liberal rate of interest and conforming in its regulations to the greatest convenience of the wage-earners; a theatre provided that is an artistic gem.

All this has been detailed so much at length that there need be to it only a passing reference. With these details in mind, imagine a perfectly equipped town of 12,000 inhabitants, built out from one central thought to a beautiful and harmonious whole. A town that is bordered with bright beds of flowers and green velvety stretches of lawn; that is shaded with trees and dotted with parks and pretty water vistas, and glimpses here and there of artistic sweeps of landscape gardening; a town where the homes, even to the most modest, are bright and wholesome and filled with pure air and light; a town, in a word, where all that is ugly, and discordant, and demoralizing, is eliminated, and all that inspires to self-respect, to thrift and to cleanliness of person and of thought is generously provided. Imagine all this, and try to picture the empty, sodden morass out of which this beautiful vision was reared, and you will then have some idea of the splendid work, in its physical aspects at least, which the far-reaching plan of Mr. Pullman has wrought.

V.

But it is the social aspects of Pullman which have been most discussed, and in the discussion of which there has been, in many cases, the most misapprehension. Indeed it is quite surprising at times to follow the well-meant reasoning from premises which do not exist to conclusions which are not so. A frequent source of error seems to lie in a failure to grasp the fundamental fact that it is upon solid *quid pro quo* business principles that the whole fabric is reared; that this is the very element upon which rests its self-sustaining strength, and from which its best benefits to humanity come; that it is from this fact that the forces which work to the general good are made self-renewing and self-perpetuating. Without a full appreciation of this pivotal proposition any attempt to know the meaning of Pullman, still more to discuss its meaning, is worse than idle. Such discussions usually lead off to such irrelevant fields of philanthropy as are occupied by the hospitals, the retreats for the aged, the maimed and the helpless. To criticise Pullman, as indeed it has been criticised, for its failure to meet the conditions of this field, is as absurd as it would be to criticise it for failure to promote the spread of the gospel among barbarous peoples.

On the business theory that the better the man, the more valuable he is to himself, just in that proportion is he better and more valuable to his employer; on this simple business theory an attempt has been made to surround the workingmen

MAIN ADMINISTRATION BUILDING.

in Pullman with such influences as would most tend to bring out
the highest and best there was in them. So far from starting
with the theory that these workingmen are weaklings to whom
things are to be given, and who must be held up and supported
lest they fall, the starting point is in exactly the opposite direction. The assumption is that the Pullman men are the best
type of American workmen, who stand solidly and firmly on
their own feet, and will work out valuable and well-rounded
lives just in proportion to their opportunities. By the investment of a large capital, it is found possible not only to give
them better conditions than they could get elsewhere, but to
give those conditions at prices wholly within their power to
pay; and yet sufficient to return a moderate interest on the
investment, and so sustain it and make it enduring. That is
the whole Pullman proposition in a nutshell. With philanthropy of the abstract sentimental sort it has nothing to do.
With the philanthropy which helps men to help themselves,
without either undermining their self-respect, or in the remotest degree touching their independence or absolute personal
liberty—with philanthropy of this type it has everything to do.

To measure the actual effect of the conditions which exist
at Pullman, it is only necessary to look at any representative
assemblage of the Pullman workmen. During the eleven years
that the town has been in existence, the Pullman workingman
has developed into a distinct type—distinct in appearance, in
tidiness of dress, in fact in all the external indications of self-
respect. Not only as compared with the majority of men
in similar walks of life do they show in their clearer complex-
ions and brighter eyes the sanitary effects of the cleanliness
and the abundance of pure air and sunlight in which they

live, but there is in their bearing and personal demeanor what seems to be a distinct reflection of the general atmosphere of order and artistic taste which permeates the entire town. It is within the mark to say that a representative gathering of Pullman workmen would be quite forty per cent. better in evidences of thrift and refinement, and in all the outward indications of a wholesome habit of life, than would a representative gathering of any corresponding group of workingmen which could be assembled elsewhere in the country. Nor do the benefits that have been brought about stop at mere external indications. The Pullman workman has a distinct rank of his own, which is recognized by employers everywhere in the United States, and which makes him universally in demand and sought after. There is, as a matter of fact, hardly a great producing center in the country, in the fields reached by the great Pullman industries, to which Pullman men have not been brought by special inducements of promotion or wages.

These things speak for themselves, just as do the six hundred thousand dollars which stand to the credit of these wage-earners in the Pullman Savings Bank, and just as does the bright border of homes which fringe the outer edge of the Pullman tract, and which represent the invested savings of nearly a thousand Pullman workmen.

The story of the town of Pullman is but a repetition on a large scale of the story of the building of the first Pullman car. The same organic solidity of structure, the same faith in the intrinsic commercial value of the beautiful, which entered into the one entered into the other. Indeed this same logical unity of purpose and allegiance to fundamental convictions, which is manifest through all the great fabric which Mr.

PUBLIC SCHOOL.

Pullman has reared during many years of labor, is the dominant, the most impressive feature of his achievement. At every step, moreover, the convictions upon which he has acted and the faiths to which he has held have been vindicated, and more than that, they have either actually wrought, or have had in them the germs of, radical benefits. The Pullman car solved the problem of long continuous railway journeys, and the town of Pullman, along new lines, gives a hope of bettering the relations of capital and labor. The issue of this last is a question of the future, but it is at least a legitimate subject of speculation, whether what the car wrought in one direction, with all its attendant and lasting benefits to humanity, may not in some sort, on a broader scale, and with benefits to humanity even more far-reaching and enduring, be repeated in the great field where the town of Pullman now stands as the advance guard of a new departure and a new idea.

In brief, the Pullman enterprise is a vast object-lesson. It has demonstrated man's capacity to improve and to appreciate improvements. It has shown that success may result from corporate action which is alike free from default, foreclosure or wreckage of any sort. It has illustrated the helpful combination of capital and labor, without strife or stultification. upon lines of mutual recognition.

ADDENDA.

STATISTICAL DATA.

The Pullman Company was organized in 1867, with a capital of $1,000,000. Its present capital stock is $74,000,000; the number of stockholders, 8,295.

The first Pullman car, the "Pioneer," was completed in 1865. There are now operated by the Company 4,095 sleeping, parlor and dining cars, under contracts covering 180,035 miles of road. The number of miles run by Pullman cars during the year ending July 31st, 1904, was 408,234,382, and the number of passengers carried was 13,312,668. The total number of employes of the Company in its operating and manufacturing departments for that year was 20,355, and the wages paid during the year, $12,570,913.55.

The longest regular unbroken run of any cars in the Pullman service is from Washington to San Francisco, 3,624 miles.

About 70,000,000 pieces of Pullman car linen are laundried annually.

The Town of Pullman has 12,000 inhabitants, and is now a part of the 33d ward of the City of Chicago. Its extreme length is about two miles in a north and south direction, and its average width one-half a mile. There are eight miles of paved streets and twelve miles of sidewalk.

The rents of dwellings range from $5.00 to $30.00 per month, the average being $11.75 a month; and there are hundreds of tenements ranging from $6.00 to $9.00 per month. These rents are considerably less than those for similar tenements with as many conveniences anywhere else in Chicago.

There are 1,400 machines in the Pullman shops. The power is furnished by 29 stationary engines, which are rated at 5,800 horse power. The principal one is the Corliss engine, rated at 2,500 horse power, which ran the machinery at the Centennial Exposition at Philadelphia, in 1876. Connected with it are 3,000 feet of main shafting and 89,400 feet of belting.

Cars of every description are made at Pullman, and the shops have a capacity for turning out each week 6 sleeping cars, 15 passenger cars and 400 freight cars.

In the shops about 54,000 tons of coal are consumed annually, and over 100,000 tons of iron and steel and about 56,500,000 feet of lumber are used.

The total amount of wages paid by the Company to its employes at Pullman from September 1st, 1880, to July 31st, 1904, was $67,174,361.05, and the value of materials used during the same period was $141,213,423.10.

The number of employes in all the industries at Pullman at this time, including women and children, is 6,915. Their average daily earnings are $2.25.

The Pullman savings bank has 6,256 depositors, and their deposits amount to $2,180,613, an average per person of $348.

Of the employes at Pullman, about 1,000 own their own homes on the borders of the Town.

PULLMAN

COLUMBIAN EXHIBITION TRAIN

www.ingramcontent.com/pod-product-compliance
Lightning Source LLC
Chambersburg PA
CBHW021542270326
41930CB00008B/1335